CW00494291

The Reign of Grace

And the End of Sin in Your Life:

An Exposition of Romans 6

"It is impossible to read or to meditate on this letter too much or too well. The more one deals with it, the more precious it becomes and the better it tastes."

Martin Luther

Preface to the Letter of St. Paul to the Romans

1522

CONTENTS

Introduction

This book is dedicated to every Christian who reads Romans 7:15 and finds that it hits too close to home: **For what I am doing, I do not understand. For what I will to do, that I do not practice; but what I hate, that I do.** This verse sums up so well the frustration of struggling against bad habits and addictions that refuse to go away. It's an awful thing to repeatedly do what you don't want to do, you feel like a visitor in your own body.

If you can relate all too well to this verse, there is good news for you. For the larger point that Paul is making in this passage is that it doesn't have to be that way for you. It's important to understand why it *can* be that way, but even more important to know that it doesn't have to.

I am not going to discuss Romans 7 in this book, however. I believe that once we have carefully looked at Romans 6, it will be clear that Romans 7:15 doesn't have to describe you at all. For Romans 6 is all about Jesus Christ reigning over you in His grace and setting you free from the sin that you hate.

I would have liked to call this book "How Not To Sin" and I think it would have sold more copies that way. But I wouldn't want to give you the impression that you are in control of the matter. You are responsible for what you do, yes, but you are not in control. You can't overcome sin without grace and you can't control grace.

Besides, Romans 6 is not so much about how not to sin as it is about *why* you're not going to sin. When you are listening to *why*, you are doing the *how*. Do you want to know how to overcome sin? By listening to Romans 6.

I don't believe that sinless perfection is attainable in this life. I believe that whoever thinks he stands should watch out lest he fall. I don't claim to be without sin. Far from it. But I have experienced the grace of God as it has set me from so much already, and I can testify that it works. I can also testify that it is beautiful, shocking, and utterly not of this world.

Romans 6 is for you just as it is for every child of God in Christ Jesus. It describes your inheritance. So please join me in taking a close look at it.

1

Context Part One: The flow of the argument in Romans

Romans 1-4

Let's take a quick look at Romans 1-4, highlighting the ideas that we will want to remember in studying Romans 6.

Romans is the apostle Paul's most comprehensive presentation of the gospel that he preached. After some introductory remarks, he begins his argument with this statement in Romans 1:16-17: **For I am not ashamed of the gospel of Christ, for it is the power of God to salvation for everyone who believes, for the Jew first and also for the Greek. For in it the righteousness of God is revealed from faith to faith; as it is written, "The just shall live by faith."**

Paul introduces the gospel as revealing a righteousness that is not revealed by any other means, including the law of Moses. It is revealed both for those who are under the law of Moses (**for the**

Jew first) and for those who are not (**and also for the Greek**).

But before he can describe this revealed righteousness he must first show that it is indeed something new, and that it is not found outside of the gospel, for then the gospel would be unnecessary. So that is what he does in Romans 1:18-3:20.

First he asserts that this revelation of righteousness is not available by general observation. Although God should be known and understood by the world He created, the sin of mankind has obscured His glory and even denied His existence. Because of sin, people do not perceive God's righteousness unless it is revealed to them in the gospel. This is Paul's argument in Romans 1:18-32.

Then Paul must demonstrate that the law of Moses did not reveal this righteousness. He begins to do this in Romans 2. In fact, he goes further and says that all moral teaching available to mankind fails to reveal the righteousness of God that is revealed in the gospel. Moral teaching gives men an understanding of what is right and wrong behavior, but it doesn't keep them from doing wrong. This is true even of the best moral teaching in the history of the world, contained in the law of Moses.

Paul argues in Romans 2:1-3:20 that although the law of Moses bears witness to the righteousness of God revealed in the gospel (which he explicitly states in 3:21) it does not produce it. It bears witness to it as a mystery, a promise of God yet to be fulfilled.

He ends this part of the argument with several verses from the Old Testament describing the sinfulness of mankind (3:10-18). The Jews, who received the Scriptures, are just as sinful as the rest of mankind. The law has not fixed the problem, so obviously something more than the law is needed.

In Romans 3:20 he says why the law of Moses does not produce the righteousness of God that is revealed only in the gospel: **Therefore by the deeds of the law no flesh will be justified in His sight, for by the law is the knowledge of sin.** This statement will be important to remember as we study Romans 6. The same law that tells you what to do condemns you for not doing it.

The law condemns you as a sinner; this is the **knowledge of sin** that Paul sees as keeping you from being justified before God. It is not just hypothetical, intellectual knowledge of sin, but guilt and shame.

You must remember this because Paul will be advocating, in Romans 6, a gospel message that can and will motivate people to live right and to do good, without adding the guilt and shame that comes from hearing the law.

Everything Paul has said in Romans 1:18-3:20 has led up to the first two small words of Romans 3:21. These two words, **But now...**, are big words for Paul. Note them. They highlight the importance of what he is about to say in the light of everything that he has already said. **But now the righteousness of God apart from the law is revealed, being witnessed by the Law and the Prophets, even the righteousness of God, through faith in Jesus Christ, to all and on all who believe.**

Paul will go on to show that the gospel he preaches is the fulfillment of what has always been taught in the Old Testament, even though this teaching was often overlooked or misunderstood. Even the Old Testament saints were righteous because of their faith in the promise of God, now fulfilled in the gospel. Even the first Jew, Abraham, was a righteous Gentile before he became a righteous Jew. So, while the gospel reveals something totally new, those who obey it are the true heirs of the saints of the Old Testament.

The place of Romans 5-8

Romans 5 begins a new section in Romans elaborating on the argument of Romans 1-4. Romans is an intricate and well thought out letter. It lends itself to many outlines, some quite elaborate. For the purpose of placing Romans 6 in its context, a good start is to see Romans divided into four main parts, with an introduction before Part One and closing remarks and greetings after Part Four.

Introduction: Romans 1:1-15

Part One: Romans 1:16-4:25

Part Two: Romans 5-8

Part Three: Romans 9-11

Part Four: Romans 12:1-15:13

Closing Remarks: Romans 15:14-33

Greetings: Romans 16

Part Four contains practical advice for the churches in Rome. Most of Paul's letters follow this pattern of theological teaching followed by practical application and exhortation.

So the theological argument is found in Parts One to Three. And Part Two, as we will see, is a little different from Parts One and Three.

Romans 1-4 is filled with direct quotations from the Old Testament. Romans 9-11 has even more. But in Romans 5-8 there are only two: one of the Ten Commandments appears in Romans 7, and Romans 8 quotes a verse from the Psalms.

Consider the number of words, in Greek, that Paul devotes to quoting the Old Testament in each part of his theological argument in Romans.

Romans 1-4: 157 words

Romans 5-8: 12 words

Romans 9-11: 366 words

This pattern reveals what Paul is doing in Romans 5-8. He has covered a lot of ground in Romans 1-4, expounding on the Scriptures and overviewing all of human history, especially in light of the distinction between Jew and Gentile. He stops to add illustrations that will make his argument easier to understand, and to answer objections that often arise when he presents this teaching. Then in Romans 9-11 he resumes his exposition of the Scriptures and finishes his theological argument.

It has often been noted that Romans 1-8 works well as an argument without adding Romans 9-11. In fact commentaries are sometimes written just on Romans 1-8. But try reading Romans without chapters 5-8. Romans 1-4 and 9-11, when read consecutively, also work well as an argument. Those sections deal with salvation history and the interpretation of the Old Testament; Romans 5-8 is more personal and practical.

But, of course, Romans is most powerful when considered in its entirety, as was intended.

2

Context Part Two: Romans 5

Reconciled to God

Romans 5:1-2 sets the tone for the next four chapters of the letter: **Therefore, having been justified by faith, we have peace with God through our Lord Jesus Christ, through whom also we have access by faith into this grace in which we stand, and rejoice in hope of the glory of God.**

It is easy to see why this section of Romans is so popular. It speaks of the personal and practical benefits of the gospel. Justification is not just a theological concept, it means real peace with God, peace that can be felt and enjoyed. Grace is not just a concept either. The gospel doesn't just tell us about grace; it gives us *access* into it. Paul is going to tell us how to live in all the blessings of the gospel.

As we have seen, he began the first section of Romans by insisting the he was **not ashamed of the gospel** (Romans 1:16). Here at the beginning of this section (Romans 5:5) he echoes that theme again: **hope does not disappoint**, that is, it gives us no reason to be ashamed.

He also touches on some themes that he will expound on in Romans 8, such as suffering, hope, love, and the Holy Spirit. Here in Romans 5:3-5 he introduces these ideas: **And not only that, but we also glory in tribulations, knowing that tribulation produces perseverance; and perseverance, character; and character, hope. Now hope does not disappoint, because the love of God has been poured out in our hearts by the Holy Spirit who was given to us.**

That gives us a taste of where Paul is headed, and he gets there in Romans 8, one of the most beloved chapters in the New Testament. But what he does next, in Romans 5:6-8, is something that he will do repeatedly. He grounds the gift of the Holy Spirit in its source, the death of Jesus.

Romans 5:6-8 continues: **For when we were still without strength, in due time Christ died for the ungodly. For scarcely for a righteous man will one die; yet perhaps for a good man someone would even dare to die. But God demonstrates His own love toward us, in that while we were still sinners, Christ died for us.**

As Paul describes the practical benefits of the gospel, he wants us to remember that it is all given to us by the death and resurrection of Jesus. This will be his emphasis in Romans 6, as we will see.

We will consider Romans 5:9-11 again in the next chapter. For now, note that Paul points both to what God has done for us in the past and to what He will do for us in the future: **Much more then, having now been justified by His blood, we shall be saved from wrath through Him. For if when we were enemies we were reconciled to God through the death of His Son, much more, having been reconciled, we shall be saved by His life.**

And then Paul points to the present, inviting us to rejoice now in what we have received: **And not only that, but we also rejoice in God through our Lord Jesus Christ, through whom we have now received the reconciliation.**

Adam and Christ

The rest of Romans 5 is an extended comparison of Christ and Adam, an illustration that has served Paul well in the past (1 Corinthians 15:20-28). The gospel of Christ is more than a clever message or a new twist on an old theme. It is a new creation, the beginning of a new human race. And Christ has influenced this new race even more than Adam influenced humanity by his transgression.

Grace is more prevalent in the new creation than death is in the old. This is a bold statement to make since the reign of death is so pervasive in this world. For example, consider just one of the ways that death rules our bodies: by requiring us to eat. We are never allowed to forget that if we go too long without eating, we will die. And that is just one of the many things we must do to keep from dying. But in the world created by Christ's resurrection, we are more aware of God's grace than we are of our own need for food. Our mortality is still a fact, but it is insignificant in the light of His eternal grace.

In Paul's comparison, Christ is not merely like Adam, He is more influential. Life doesn't just reign instead of death, it reigns more powerfully. Grace doesn't just deal with condemnation, it overwhelms it.

Here is Paul repeatedly making this contrast in Romans 5:12-21:

Therefore, just as through one man sin entered the world, and death through sin, and thus death spread to all men, because all sinned—(For until the law sin was in the world, but sin is not imputed when there is no law. Nevertheless death reigned from Adam to Moses, even other those who had not sinned according to the likeness of the transgression of Adam, who is a type of Him who was to come.

But the free gift is not like the offense. For if by the one man's offense many died, much more the grace of God and the gift by the grace of the one Man, Jesus Christ, abounded to many.

And the gift is not like that which came through the one who sinned. For the judgment which came from one offense resulted in condemnation, but the free gift which came from many offenses resulted in justification.

For if by the one man's offense death reigned through the one, much more those who receive abundance of grace and of the gift of righteousness will reign in life through the One, Jesus Christ.)

Therefore, as through one man's offense judgment came to all men, resulting in condemnation, even so through one Man's righteous act the free gift came to all men, resulting in justification of life.

For as by one man's disobedience many were made sinners, so also by one Man's obedience many will be made righteous.

Moreover the law entered that the offense might abound.

But where sin abounded, grace abounded much more, so that as sin reigned in death, even so grace might reign through righteousness to eternal life through Jesus Christ our Lord.

Paul makes such grand claims for his gospel. It is so much more than just a new way to interpret the Scriptures. It's more than a continuation, on a larger scale, of what God has always been doing.

Paul knows that he has to defend these claims, and that the best proof for them is that the gospel works in people's lives. So, beginning in Romans 6, he shows how his gospel works in the real world.

3

"Shall We Continue in Sin": Romans 6:1

The Question that Always Gets Asked

Is Paul's gospel really something new? Is it as new as he says it is? After all, the saints of the Old Testament were under the law of Moses yet they knew the grace and mercy of God. Paul acknowledged this already in Romans 3:25, saying that **in His forbearance God had passed over the sins that were previously committed** so that He might demonstrate His righteousness in this new way.

But now God has done the new thing. He has raised Jesus from the dead. We are now New Testament saints, but how different is our experience of grace?

Those Old Testament saints lived in the grace of what God was going to do for them in the future, which remained a mystery. So do God's people now just live in the grace of what God did for them in the past, which still remains somewhat of a mystery? Is the situation really all that different now?

Paul says yes, there is literally a world of difference. The future age has already come with the resurrection of Jesus and the gift of the Holy Spirit. The reign of grace has begun and it really is a whole new world. And this world, how it came about and how it operates, is not meant to be mysterious to us.

The test of this claim is in the lives of those who believe it. If things are really different now people will not go on living in the same old way. Either grace will really change people or Paul is making stuff up.

So in Romans 6:1 Paul asks the question: **What shall we say then? Shall we continue in sin that grace may abound?** He has heard this objection before, which is why he is raising it himself. He knows it will be asked.

On the surface this question is a concern that others will abuse the message of grace. The fear is that if you proclaim that grace reigns it will dull people's consciences and make them think they are getting away with sin.

Paul has already addressed this problem in Romans 3:1-8. Some drew the following conclusion from Paul's gospel: **Let us do evil that good may come**. There will always be people who draw that conclusion. Paul can't say much more about them than that **their condemnation is just**. Grace is not going to work for them—not yet anyway. They are still under the law.

The gospel will inevitably be abused and distorted. The solution is not to preach it less but to preach it more clearly. The best answer to a wrong understanding of grace is the right understanding. People abuse the teaching of grace because they have never understood it.

But when it's not abused, does it work? That's the really important question. In Romans 6 Paul is addressing the concerns of people who don't want to abuse the gospel, but are afraid that they will, afraid that, no matter how good their intentions are, they will inevitably abuse grace, because Paul is wrong about its effectiveness.

So Romans 6 begins Paul's defense of the practical effectiveness of his gospel. Can people trust the message of grace to really change them, or will they stay the same; will they continue in sin?

Paul's Answer

Consider two common answers to this question that Paul could have given. First, he could have appealed to the law, saying, "You'd better not sin because it is wrong and you will suffer the consequences." If he said that he would be telling the truth but not saying anything new. Paul claims that he has a new message for a new age. He can't fall back on the law now; it would undermine his whole argument and confirm the suspicion of the skeptics that the gospel is just another message among many.

The law can be used to motivate people, but not without an inevitable measure of guilt and fear. Remember that Romans 3:20 says that **by the law is the knowledge of sin**. This knowledge of sin includes guilt and fear. That is not a bad thing. Sinners are guilty and should fear God. But it's not a new thing either.

Is there a motivation not to sin that doesn't remind us that we're already sinners, that doesn't condemn us? If Paul's teaching about being dead to the old world of sin and renewed in God's image is true, then there must be a way to talk to that new person as a new person. The law works great to address sinners, warning and condemning them. But how does the *gospel* keep us from sin?

The second answer that Paul could have given goes something like this: "You will do good and avoid sin out of thankfulness to God. Good works are your way of thanking Him for grace."

That's all well and good, but what if I'm not thankful? That may sound pessimistic, but it is the very nature of sin not to appreciate God and what He does for us. So it is just like a sinner to be ungrateful for the grace of the gospel.

The question is, "What if grace doesn't change me?" No doubt I will do good works and avoid sin if I am thankful to God, but thankfulness is part of the change. What if grace leaves me in my ingratitude and sin? That is the question Paul has to answer in Romans 6.

Paul gives his answer in Romans 6:2-14. In these 13 verses he makes, by my count, six direct references to Christ's death, four to His resurrection, and at least seven to the special relationship that the believer has to that death and resurrection. Paul's answer is hard to miss.

Grace is the death and resurrection of Jesus Christ at work in your life. How can it *not* work? If the death and resurrection of Jesus Christ is weak and ineffective when it comes to ending your sinful habits and producing gratitude in your heart, you've got worse problems than the prospect of not being changed. You are going to need grace to do much bigger jobs than just breaking your bad habits. If grace is so weak that it can't change you, how is it going to save you?

But although personal transformation is just part of the larger work that grace does in a believer's life, it can be the hardest part to believe. Christians often put more confidence in the power of grace to save them than its power to change them. This is because it is easier to believe God about something we can't see than about something we can.

Paul has already addressed this problem earlier in Romans. Let's take another look at Romans 5:9-10. He has been explicating his doctrine of justification by faith. He promises that faith gives us confidence that we will be saved from wrath, that is, the future wrath of God that is coming on the whole world because of sin: **Much more then, having now been justified by His blood, we shall be saved from wrath through Him. For if, when we were enemies, we were reconciled to God through the death of His Son, much more, having been reconciled, we shall be saved by His life.**

On Judgment Day it will be too late for you to do anything. You will stand before God and the outcome will be out of your hands. This is something that you cannot see or imagine. But because of Jesus you can have confidence that you will be saved from wrath on that Day.

You know that you will be utterly powerless on Judgment Day, a Day that you do not yet see. But when it comes to the matter of grace changing your life today, then you are dealing with something that you can see very clearly and about which you don't seem to be utterly powerless. It can be harder to believe.

But Paul goes on to say that the same grace that will save you from what you cannot see (the wrath of God on Judgment Day) will also save you from what you can clearly see (your sinful self today). After affirming that we are saved from future wrath he says: ***And not only that, but* we also rejoice in God through our Lord Jesus Christ through whom *we have now received* the reconciliation**. (Romans 5:11, emphasis added) The blood of Jesus affects not only future salvation, but daily salvation. The death and resurrection of Jesus Christ not only works on Judgment Day, it works now.

4

Baptism: Romans 6:2-5

Yesterday, Today, and Forever

In Romans 6:2-5 Paul begins to answer the question whether grace will allow us to continue sinning: **Certainly not! How shall we who died to sin live any longer in it? Or do you not know that as many of us as were baptized into Christ Jesus were baptized into His death? Therefore we were buried with Him through baptism into death, that just as Christ was raised from the dead by the glory of the Father, even so we also should walk in newness of life. For if we have been united together in the likeness of His death, certainly we shall also be in the likeness of His resurrection...**

When explaining why grace works to keep believer's from sinning, Paul starts with baptism. That's how important and powerful he considered baptism to be. But the generations that followed Paul must have, for the most part, misunderstood him on this point, because many in the early church lacked his confidence in the practical effectiveness of baptism.

Early church history shows that baptism was sometimes taught and understood in such a manner that believers were actually reluctant to be baptized. Baptism was thought to deal effectively with all sins that had been committed in the past, but not sins that may be committed in the future (especially the more serious sins). Since people were concerned about sins committed after baptism, they sometimes waited until they were on their death beds to be baptized, because then they would not have the time or the energy to sin again.

People with such concerns were right that baptism kills the old person and raises the new. But they were wrong in that they saw baptism strictly as a past event and thought that all of its killing power was used up in one day. The problem was how they divided the old from the new in a linear fashion instead of realizing that the division of the old from the new is the ongoing work of the Spirit in a believer's life.

This view of baptism was similar to the way that the 18th century Deists viewed the creation of the world. Deists thought that God made the world and set up the rules by which it operates, and then left it alone and no longer gets involved with His creation, in fact He might not even be paying attention. Similarly, God was seen as being active in baptism on the day it happened, and that one day of activity would have to last a lifetime.

Another way to say it is that the early church saw baptism as a wedding, while Paul saw it as a marriage. A wedding ceremony can last several hours, but a marriage can last for decades.

Baptism joins you to the living Christ, so it is always working in your life, killing the old and raising the new. The fear that grace won't work is part of the fear that the old man experiences as he is plunged into the death of Christ. Christ is alive and active in your life to daily drown that fear in the waters of your baptism.

Forgiveness and Deliverance

Although Christians today do not delay baptism until they are about to die, they often have similar attitudes about grace in general. They agree when they hear teaching about the life-changing power of grace, but when it comes down to it they are often afraid to try, because if it doesn't work there will be nothing left to believe in.

If grace failed it would be a terrible disappointment, so people don't really put grace to the test so that they won't lose their faith in it. They would rather believe in an untested grace than risk it all to experience the real thing. So, to protect grace from failure, they make everything depend on themselves.

Another thing that modern Christians have in common with those early, baptism-delaying Christians, is that they are often more confident that grace works for past sins than for future sins.

If we were told that baptism includes the forgiveness of future sins, it would seem like baptism gives us a license to sin, the very fear that Paul was addressing in Romans 6. On the other hand, if baptism only works for past sins, we need a new source of grace to deal with future sins. But baptism joins us to the resurrected Jesus, the only source of grace we will ever need.

But what about that license to sin? It's like a monster lurking around every corner. But if you truly understand grace, you will not be afraid of it. The same grace that forgives your future sins renders you powerless to commit them. It is knowing and understanding that he died for them that delivers you from doing them.

When Jesus died for your sins, they were *all* in the future, but that didn't stop him. He knew what He was doing. He didn't die just to forgive your sins, he died to prevent them. He brought them to an end in His death. You only sinned in the past because you didn't know this. You will sin in the future only to the extent that you forget this. Because if you understand this, as Paul said, how can you keep sinning?

Christians who delay baptism or who fear grace understand correctly that they have a strong inclination to sin. We human beings just can't get enough of sin, no matter how hard we try. Isaiah 57:10 speaks of those who have sinned so much but still found the energy to sin some more: **You are wearied in the length of your way; Yet you did not say, 'There is no hope.' You have found the life of your hand; Therefore you were not grieved**.

As sinners, we can never sin enough. We are like an alcoholic who thinks he can drink so much in one night that he will never need another drink, but finds that the craving returns the next day.

It's as if we have a bank account of sin that never runs out, we can always go to the bank and withdraw some more sin—until one day you go to the bank and find that your account is empty; somebody robbed you and spent all your sins before you could get to them.

That's what Jesus did. If you accept that he died for the forgiveness of all your future sins, then you will understand that he also took them away. Does that mean that He died for sins that you will never actually commit? No, it means He died not just for a certain number of sins, but for you, the sinner.

Of course, if you don't actually commit those future sins, then they don't exist to be forgiven. But *why* aren't you going to commit them? Because you're afraid you might exhaust the grace of God? That's not going to work. Because being forgiven by God has changed you? Yes, but how is it going to change you if you're afraid it might run out? The grace that is going to change you will be the grace that also convinces you that the Almighty God,who sees the end from the beginning, has truly taken the matter into His own hands.

As we will consider in the next chapter, Paul says in Romans 6:6 that **our old man was crucified with Him, that the body of sin might be done away with, that we should no longer be slaves of sin**. Baptism works because the cross works. It kills sin. The "body of sin" is broken, out of order, useless.

Grace means that you can finally be tired of sinning, that your energy for sin is finally spent; there's no life in it anymore. After suffering the same consequences over and over again for doing what you knew was foolish, you can stop. The alcoholic can stop drinking. The sinner is broke, with no sin left in his account, past or future.

5

Reigning in Life: Romans 6:6-8

Sharing His Justification

In Romans 6:6 Paul continues to establish the death and resurrection of Jesus Christ as the reason that grace works in a believer's life: **...knowing this, that our old man was crucified with Him, that the body of sin might be done away with, that we should no longer be slaves of sin**.

Grace is an historical fact, not just an abstract concept. Some of the Romans to whom Paul was writing were born after Christ was crucified. All believers on earth today were born many years afterward. Nevertheless we were killed with Christ on the cross. That is how much the matter is out of our hands: it happened before we were born.

And it happened to us together. Paul refers to our old *man,* not our old *men*. It was our common human nature that we inherited from Adam that was crucified with Jesus.

Romans 6:7 continues: **For he who has died has been freed from sin**. The New King James Version here renders this verse using *he* with a small case *h,* not a capital *H.* That would indicate that the statement is not referring to Jesus specifically, but to whoever dies, as being freed from sin by dying. I doubt, however, that this is the correct way to translate the verse.

There is nothing about death in and of itself that frees anyone from sin. Yes, it's an observable fact that a dead person cannot sin anymore simply because he is dead. But that does not mean that he is free from sin, and I doubt that Paul is appealing to this common sense principle, especially because the word he uses for *freed* in this verse is the same word that he often uses to mean *justified.*

Jesus said in John 8:21, **I am going away, and you will seek Me, and will die in your sin**. He said later, in John 8:34, that **whoever commits sin is a slave of sin**. Death itself would not free these slaves who died in their sin. On the contrary, it would make their slavery permanent.

Let me translate Romans 6:7 with a capital *H*: **For *He* who has died has been freed [justified] from sin**. Christ, the One whose death we share, was justified from sin when He was raised from the dead. Because He died sinless, death could not hold Him (Acts 2:24). His resurrection was proof of His sinlessness, and in that sense He was justified from sin when He was raised from the dead. We died His death with Him. He took our sins to the grave and left them there. He now shares His resurrection and justification and righteousness with us.

Replacing Death

Paul continues in Romans 6:8, **Now if we have died with Christ, we believe that we shall also live with Him...** Here again I have to take issue with the New King James Version (and most other versions). The problem is with that little word *if*. *If* implies uncertainty, but Paul is talking about something that has already happened, not something that might happen. Romans 6:8 would be better translated with *since* or *because*: **Now *since* we have died with Christ, we believe that we shall also live with Him...**

The life we live with Him starts now. Just as Christ died for you before you were born, you were also raised from the dead with Him before you were born. When He was declared sinless, so were you. Death could not hold Him, and neither, by the grace of God, can it hold you. You can't stay dead. The righteousness of God will not allow it and death itself is not able to keep you.

And you can walk in this confidence now because grace is reigning in your life. Remember Romans 5:20-21: **But where sin abounded, grace abounded much more, so that as sin reigned in death, even so grace might reign through righteousness**

to eternal life through Jesus Christ our Lord. This is happening to you right now.

Remember also Romans 5:17, where, contrasting Christ and Adam, Paul said this: **For if by the one man's offense death reigned through the one, much more those who receive abundance of grace and of the gift of righteousness will reign in life through the One, Jesus Christ**.

Notice how Paul puts you, the receiver of grace, right into the middle of the equation. You are not on the sidelines. In this whole passage (Romans 5:12-21) Paul makes repeated comparisons: Adam and Christ, sin and righteousness, etc. Notice that in verse 17 he compares the reign of death on the one hand with the reign of life on the other hand. But he doesn't just say, "once death reigned, now life reigns." He puts you in there: "once death reigned, but now *those who receive grace* reign in life." When you receive grace, you reign instead of death.

Death didn't just reign as an abstract concept; it made its reign known in practical and tangible ways. So also life now reigns in grace *through you*. You are the opposite of death. Grace makes you that way. But, as a manifestation of life, you are not an equal opposite, for life and death are not like yin and yang, but you are a much more powerful opposing force. Such is the power of grace in your life.

6

Knowledge of His Glory: Romans 6:9-14

Know Christ, Know Yourself

In Romans 6:3-10, Paul looks at the effect that the death and resurrection of Jesus has on a believer from three angles: baptism, the cross, and the living Christ. Below is Romans 6:3-10 divided into these three reasons why grace works. They are each introduced by Paul's use of the word *know*, for he is describing a threefold knowledge of grace.

***Or do you not know that* as many of us as were baptized into Christ Jesus were baptized into His death? Therefore we were buried with Him through baptism into death, that just as Christ was raised from the dead by the glory of the Father, even so we should walk in newness of life. For if we have been united together in the likeness of His death, certainly we also shall be in the likeness of His resurrection,**

knowing this, **that our old man was crucified with Him, that the body of sin might be done away with, that we should no longer be slaves of sin. For He who has died has been freed from sin. Now since we died with Christ, we believe that we shall also live with Him,**

knowing that **Christ, having been raised from the dead, dies no more. Death no longer has dominion over Him. For the death that He died, He died to sin once for all; but the life that He lives, He lives to God.**

The first knowledge is through baptism, which is an event in the life of the believer that bears witness to God's work in that person. The second knowledge is outside of the life of the believer, it is the crucifixion of Jesus Christ. It is rooted in the work of God in world history. The third knowledge of grace transcends even world history. It is knowledge of the living Christ. It is the life He lives now, which He lives to God for us. He lives to make grace work. For this reason we can have unshakable confidence that grace will change us.

In Romans 6:11-14 Paul starts to talk about the personal benefits of this kind of knowledge: **Likewise you also, reckon yourselves to be dead indeed to sin, but alive to God in Christ Jesus our Lord. Therefore do not let sin reign in your mortal body, that you should obey it in its lusts. And do not present your members as instruments of unrighteousness to sin,**

but present yourselves to God as being alive from the dead, and your members as instruments of righteousness to God. For sin shall not have dominion over you, for you are not under law but under grace.

If you are task-oriented like me, you will be excited when you get to verses 11-13, because they give you something to do. "Finally," you might say, "Paul is telling me what to do. In fact he is giving me two things to do: *reckon* and *present*. If I can just figure out how to do those two things I'll never sin again."

If, on the other hand, you are relationship-oriented, you will still be pondering verses 3-10, and you'll be better off. Don't rush past those verses to the part that gives you something to do. The power that changes you is in the relationship.

Reckoning (or considering) yourself dead to sin is a point of view that comes as a result of seeing Christ crucified for you and raised from the dead. Think long and hard about what Paul says in verses 3-10 and the reckoning will be automatic. If not, go back and think about it some

more.

Put Yourself in Perspective

It is only after Paul has clearly portrayed Christ in His freedom and glory that he says, "you also think of yourselves in the same way." It is easy to think of yourself as dead to sin and alive to God once you have seen Christ that way. When you see yourself in the light of the knowledge of His glory, grace works.

It may seem counter-intuitive, but the more you exalt Christ in your thinking, the easier it is to picture yourself like Him. The greater your esteem for His freedom and the more you stand in awe of it, the easier it will be to consider yourself free from sin and alive to God in the same manner. The more you magnify Christ in relation to sin and death and the universe, the more accurate your vision of Him will be, and also your vision of yourself. It is easy to see yourself as free from unrighteous behavior in the light of His glory. The greater He is to you, the greater is His power to make you like Him.

If, on the other hand, you minimize Him, it will be harder to consider yourself like Him. If you think of Him as merely the most wise and good man who ever lived, the best moral example to follow, then you will never be like Him at all.

It is as the conqueror of death and evil—the master of every imaginable universe, whose greatness cannot be measured—that He makes you like Him. It is your destiny to be conformed to His image, and He fulfills this destiny for you by ruling over you in His grace.

But maybe you're not excited when you get to the part where Paul tells you what to do. Maybe you're disappointed. After all that talk about grace is he now putting all the responsibility on you and your ability to reckon and present? Is grace just another form of the law after all?

No. Just because you do some stuff doesn't mean you're not under grace anymore. Grace doesn't mean the lack of all activity. And besides, Paul only tells the Romans that they need to deny sin and present themselves to God after listing some of the things that grace has done for them that they could not do themselves.

You cannot join yourself to Christ in baptism. You cannot unite yourself to Him in His death so as to make it your death as well. You cannot make Christ alive today. You can't come close to doing any of those things, and grace did it all for you. Jesus does it.

In light of all of this grace, Paul's exhortation to deny sin's reign and present yourself to God need not fall upon you like the heavy burden of the law. The law brings uncertainty. Grace gives certainty, but grace is not the absence of work. Grace is work, but it is delightful work because of the confident expectation of success.

This command, in the light of so much grace, is like healing a crippled man and telling him to walk. He is not going to complain that you are giving him work to do.

Reckoning yourself dead to sin flows naturally out of the knowledge of the glory of His grace. Focus on developing that knowledge. As for the other command, to present yourself to God, we will consider it in the next chapter because Paul elaborates on it in the rest of Romans 6.

7

Present Yourselves Slaves: Romans 6:15-18

How to Present Yourself

The second half of Romans 6 is introduced by another rhetorical question.

What then? Shall we sin because we are not under law but under grace? Certainly not! Do you not know that to whom you present yourselves slaves to obey, you are that one's slaves whom you obey, whether of sin leading to death, or of obedience leading to righteousness?

The thing you need to know about presenting yourself is that you're already doing it. Every day you present yourself and you obey. Everybody does. You can't *not* do it. You do it just by living your life.

But to present and to obey are not necessarily two steps. In fact they usually aren't. Whether you sin or do good, you are not usually aware of a conscious decision that you made that could be considered a presentation of yourself to one master or another. In most cases the obedience *is* the presentation. It's all one step. You just do what you do, and by doing it, you are presenting yourself to your master.

By committing a sin you are presenting yourself as a slave. By doing a righteous act you are also demonstrating your slavery to righteousness. Your actions demonstrate your loyalty.

And when are you doing these acts of slavery? 20% of the time? Just in the afternoon? Just on the weekends? The answer is all the time. Again, you do it just by living your life. You can't opt out.

Most people don't believe this because they picture themselves as neutral agents in a kind of in-between position, a position from which they can deliberate and choose what side they are going to serve. And in most of life, this works.

When two armies are at war there is often an area of land between them that is not yet claimed by either army. This is called "no man's land." During the legendary Christmas truce of 1914, English and German soldiers stopped fighting one another, met in the "no man's land" between their armies, traded goods, sang Christmas carols, and even played soccer.

This may be possible during human wars, but God and the devil fight a different kind of battle. There is no space between sin and righteousness.

These two masters are relentless and you must always do the bidding of one or the other.

How to Do Works

So you present yourself to your master by your works. But what you might consider your works to be and what the Bible calls works are not necessarily the same. When the New Testament speaks of "works," it must be understood in the context of this constant conflict between the kingdom of light and the kingdom of darkness. From a spiritual point of view, you are always doing works. Works are not 20% of your life. Works is human behavior. Whatever you do or don't do, that's your works. Works is not extra stuff you do on the side.

Humans were made to work and they are always working. They were made to bear fruit and so they do. Even if you are intentionally doing nothing, that's your work. You are bearing the fruit of laziness.

So you are always working, and that work serves one of two masters. If that thought overwhelms you with pressure and responsibility, good for you. You are in a position to be even more overwhelmed by the reign of grace over your life, because grace replaces every bit of that pressure.

Look again at Romans 6:16. It may appear that Paul has been a bit sloppy with his analogy: **Do you not know that to whom you present your-**

selves slaves to obey, you are that one's slaves whom you obey, whether of sin leading to death, or of obedience leading to righteousness? He says you have to obey one of two masters. The choice is this: obey sin or obey obedience. But does it make sense to tell people to obey obedience? Isn't that like saying, "listen to listening"?

Is "obey obedience" the result of a sloppy metaphor? I don't think so. I think Paul has two different obediences in view here: yours and Christ's. One is perfect; the other, not so much. But that is what you are ultimately a slave to obey. You don't obey rules or principles or laws, at least not directly. You obey Christ's obedience. He comes between you and every law, obeying it perfectly. You obey the rules for His sake. You are a slave to His perfection; and His perfection means grace for you.

Paul will go on, in verses 17-18, to refer to Christ's perfect obedience as a form of doctrine. In other words, the teaching, the gospel of grace, is Christ-shaped: **But God be thanked that though you were slaves of sin, yet you obeyed from the heart that form of doctrine to which you were delivered. And having been set free from sin, you became slaves of righteousness.**

He is continuing with his slavery metaphor, painting a picture of a slave who loves his new master so much that he works for him because he wants to, not because he has to. This kind of scenario wouldn't seem that far-fetched to the Roman believers. It was something that made sense to them. The Jewish believers in Rome would also remember that the Old Testament made provision for such situations, anticipating that slaves would sometimes come to love their masters and not want to leave them. (see Exodus 21:1-6 and Deuteronomy 15:16-17)

Paul's task was to bring the gospel to people. But it was also to bring people to the gospel, to deliver them over as slaves to a new master. But slavery to the perfect obedience of Christ is different from any other kind of slavery. In fact, from the point of view of being ruled by grace, it isn't slavery at all, as we will see in the next chapter.

8

Righteousness unto Holiness: Romans 6:19-23

The Holy Snowball Effect

At this point Paul has pushed his slavery metaphor so far that he has to admit, before going even further with it, that it's not perfect. All metaphors have their limitations, so he interjects this disclaimer: **I speak in human terms because of the weakness of your flesh.**

The obedience of faith in Christ is actually the opposite of slavery. It is the only true freedom. But as human beings we are so far from really understanding true freedom that we don't recognize it when we see it. We need to learn all over again, taught by the Holy Spirit. Even these Roman saints, the recipients of this profound letter, had this weakness. Paul had to call freedom slavery so that they could better understand it.

So sticking with his slavery metaphor, Paul introduces some really good news. Once grace starts working in your life it builds momentum. First it takes over your life, then it increases and abounds.

Romans 6:19 continues: **For just as you presented your members as slaves of uncleanness, and of lawlessness leading to more lawlessness, so now present your members as slaves of righteousness for holiness.**

There is a kind of momentum in doing wrong. You can call it a slippery slope. Paul calls it **lawlessness leading to more lawlessness.** Small misdeeds lead to bigger ones. Breaking small rules and getting away with it makes it easier to break some big rules.

The good news is that this kind of momentum works for righteous behavior as well. For although Christians still tend to think of their works as neutral, their faith in Christ makes them good. That means that even the little things they do on a daily basis, like brushing their teeth and making their beds, are works of righteousness.

Let's take a look back at Romans 5:19: **For as by one man's disobedience many were made sinners, so also by one Man's obedience many will be made righteous**. When Paul says that many were *made* sinners and many were *made* righteous, he is literally saying that they were *appointed* as such. In Adam they were put into a position of enmity against God. From that position everything they did was sin. But those who are in

Christ have been put into a position from which everything they do is righteous.

Now let's look ahead to Romans 14:23. Paul is addressing conflicts between believers about what foods should and should not be eaten. His counsel is that each person must follow their own conscience. If certain foods trouble one's conscience, he or she shouldn't eat them: **But he who doubts is condemned if he eats, because he does not eat from faith; for whatever is not from faith is sin.**

Whatever is not from faith is sin, so these troubled believers should follow their consciences (even if Paul himself sees it as a weakness). But the converse of that principle is also true: whatever *is* from faith is *not* a sin. To act from faith is to act from that position that Christ has put you in, from which whatever you do, however small and seemingly insignificant, is righteous.

Your faith in Christ will not lead you into sin. From that righteous position to which you are appointed you will not break one of the Ten Commandments. If you do, you are doing it from your former position as a sinner. From faith you can only do good.

That means that the little things you do every day are good works. That doesn't mean you don't still do the big things, but when you do them, it is as a natural extension of your daily life. If you think of your daily routine as righteous and full of good works, it will lead to greater works of righteousness. Living under grace will become a kind of habit. Good works will be natural, and it will be more and more unnatural for you to sin.

Jesus spoke in the Sermon on the Mount about living your life with confidence that God sees everything you do. The New American Standard Bible gives a good translation of Matthew 6:1: **Beware of practicing your righteousness before men to be noticed by them; otherwise you have no reward with your Father who is in heaven.** What other translations refer to as "doing good deeds," the NASB calls, "practicing righteousness."

The disciples hearing the Sermon on the Mount did not yet understand how Jesus was going to give them the gift of righteousness, but Jesus understood. He expected them to give to the poor, pray, and fast. He did not speak of this as earning their righteousness or even proving their righteousness, but of practicing it. That is, exercising what they already have, using the gift God has given them.

If you brush your teeth in the morning with faith that you are pleasing to God for Christ's sake, then you have already begun practicing your righteousness. That doesn't mean you won't also give to the poor, pray, and fast. It means you will have righteous momentum that will make these things easier to do.

But won't you just brush your teeth, make your bed, and get all complacent and self-satisfied? Certainly not! Grace doesn't work that way. It's not a license to sin and it's not a license to be lazy either.

Doing Your Duty v. Extra Credit

Paul continues in Romans 6:20: **For when you were slaves of sin, you were free in regard to righteousness.** This doesn't mean that they never did anything good until they became Christians. Everyone does at least of little bit of good for the world around them. But when it came to righteous deeds, they thought of themselves as free agents who could do or not do them according to how they felt.

When I was in college a man who lived near the school was auditing a class. He was not a student at that college but he enjoyed the subject so he came to class sometimes just to listen. But sometimes he didn't come, and when it was time to take the test, he wasn't there. Those of us who were students, however, had to take the test.

This is how slaves of sin see themselves when it comes to righteousness. They think they are auditing the class. They don't think that they will be tested. This is an illusion.

Such people, when they do something good, think it's a big deal. After all, so they think, they didn't have to do anything; they were **free with regard to righteousness**.

Jesus warned against such an attitude in Luke 17:7-10: **And which of you, having a servant plowing or tending sheep, will say to him when he has come in from the field, "Come at once and sit down to eat"? But will he not rather say to him, "Prepare something for my supper, and gird yourself and serve me till I have eaten and drunk, and afterward you will eat and drink"? Does he thank that servant because he did the things that were commanded him? I think not. So likewise you, when you have done all those things which you are commanded, say, "We are unprofitable servants. We have done what was our duty to do**."

If you are under the law this parable will fill you with dread, for how can you ever know if you did **all those things which you are commanded**? But if you are under grace, it means that no matter how much good you do, it's just your normal routine. You do your works by living your life with faith in Jesus Christ and doing what you see needs to be done. You don't do what you do to impress God, which is, after all, impossible.

In Romans 6:21 Paul, still reminding the Romans of their former lives, asks them, **What fruit did you have then in the things of which you are now ashamed? For the end of those things is death.**

Here's some good advice for those of us who used to enjoy sinning. Learn how to remember sin. There is a right way and a wrong way. People often remember having fun while sinning, but they don't remember the pain it caused. This is the same way that they look at sin in the future; they think that it will be fun and not painful. But Paul says don't remember the fun, remember the fruit. And the fruit of sin is always misery and pain.

Sin always brings pain. If you remember your sins correctly, you will know that this is true. Sin brings death, not only at the end of your life but during your life. It kills your joy and your peace. Romans 6 ends with Paul, in verses 22-23, reminding us of this and contrasting it with the gift of God's grace.

But now having been set free from sin, and having become slaves of God, you have your fruit to holiness, and the end, everlasting life. For the wages of sin is death, but the gift of God is eternal life in Christ Jesus our Lord.

Conclusion

In this life you are always able to sin. There is no state of perfection from which you cannot fall. Such perfection is not taught in Romans 6 or anywhere else in the Bible. You will always need to be warned about the danger of sin, so the law remains until Jesus returns.

The New Testament does teach, however, that you can live free of persistent bad habits that cause you to do what you know is wrong. Grace will break all of these habits. You may have to make drastic changes in your life and environment. Things may get difficult for a while. But everything that dares to exercise power over you will be broken by the reign of God's grace.

If you really want to change you will. If you're not sure how much you really want to change, keep meditating on the death and resurrection of Jesus Christ and what it means for your life. That's where the grace is and that's where the power comes from.

Let me leave you with one last thought, for in your struggle against sin you may be tempted to wonder whether grace is doing anything at all or if you are on your own. If it seems to you that you are left to your own efforts, consider something that God said to Moses once.

Remember when God appeared to Moses in the burning bush. He gave Moses a very hard task: to convince Pharaoh to let the Israelites go and to get the Israelites to follow him. He was reluctant. God said to him: **I will certainly be with you. And this shall be a sign to you that I have sent you: When you have brought the people out of Egypt, you shall serve God on this mountain**. (Exodus 3:12)

It turned out to be hard work dealing with the Israelites and with Pharaoh. At times it didn't look like Moses would succeed. But God assured him that after he had succeeded, he would worship God on Mt. Sinai, and that would be the sign that God had sent him.

I am sure that Moses would have liked that sign to come during his struggle, not after he was successful. But we know, of course, that he did have many astounding signs that God was with him during his dealing with Pharaoh, like turning his staff into a snake. These were signs given in the heat of battle. The worship at the mountain was a sign given from the perspective of victory.

If you are serious about laying aside every weight and sin that entangles, and running the race set before you, God will certainly be with you. You may be tempted to wonder if you are struggling in vain, but deliverance will come. And when it does you will worship God and know that He was with you all along and your deliverance was all by His grace.

In the midst of the struggle this might not be so clear to you. Chalk it up to the fog of war. In your victory, however, you will understand that it was His forgiveness and mercy that changed you, that beyond all guilt and shame His voice of love was ever speaking to you, recreating you in His image.

May Christ rule over you in His grace now and forever. Peace be with you.

About the Author

Joshua Nickel was born on August 14, 1973. He is currently living somewhere with his wife and children.

Free written and audio material is available at JoshuaNickel.com, and you can subscribe by email to be notified of when new books are published.

The Language of Grace

Learning to Hear the Gospel Well

The same grace of God in Jesus Christ that gives you eternal life also makes your present life more abundant.

The grace of God makes problems easier to solve, trials easier to bear, and people easier to love.

And while the riches of His grace are unsearchable and its depths unfathomable, there are simple things that you can do to make sure that you are experiencing grace in a practical and effective way.

You need to hear God speak His grace to you through the gospel every day. Proverbs 2:2 tells us to make our ears attentive to wisdom and incline our hearts to understanding.

You can train the ears of your heart to hear the language of grace, but to do so, you also need to hear the language of the law. You need to be bilingual, hearing both languages and keeping them distinct from one another in your heart.

I don't want to reach the end of my life and discover that I could have lived in much more of the grace of God than I ever did. I am learning to hear the gospel well and I invite you to join me.

I have started a blog at TheLanguageOfGrace.net. Every week I am writing about what I have learned about living under the reign of God's grace. Visit my blog to read articles and/or sign up to receive an article every Friday by email.

On the pages that follow is the first post from TheLanguageOfGrace.net.

Grace Not Only Saves Us, It Also Teaches Us How to Live

But, according to Paul's summary in Titus 2:11-13 it teaches us something that the law also taught. So why do we need two teachers?

"For the grace of God that brings salvation has appeared to all men, teaching us that, denying ungodliness and worldly lusts, we should live soberly, righteously, and godly in the present age, looking for the blessed hope and glorious appearing of our great God and Savior Jesus Christ." (Titus 2:11-13)

The law of Moses also instructed the Israelites to live godly lives and to wait for their Messiah, just as Paul, in Titus, says that we are to do. The difference is that they waited for Christ's first coming and we for His second coming.

Of course grace does give us new information. But grace differs from the law not just in what it says, but in how effective it is at saying the same things. Yes, the law taught the people how to live, but it was like a substitute teacher that could do little more than keep the children under control until their regular teacher returned. The law taught the same subject, just not as well as grace teaches it.

I want to be taught by grace; not because it's easier, but because it works better. It is the teaching that brings about real change. Actually, I want to learn from both grace and law, for God speaks to His children in both ways, using both teachers.

Law and Grace Are not Only Two Different Teachers, They Are Two Different Languages

And it seems that the language of law is easier to hear. In fact, sometimes when God speaks grace we hear law. It takes practice and effort not to turn God's grace into another law.

One reason for this is that the language of law is what we are used to hearing and what makes more sense in this world. The language of grace, on the other hand, doesn't describe this world, but creates a new world for us to live in.

Another reason that the language of law is easier to hear is that it gives us a measure of control, or at least the illusion of control. The language of grace shatters that illusion.

Another reason is that we actually fear the grace of God, sometimes even as much as we long for it. In this blog I will be examining exactly why this is so: why God's children have a hard time hearing Him when He speaks grace to us, and why we fear His grace.

I will also be considering why and how grace works. It *is* a better teacher.

The language of grace is God's creative voice at work in the world today. It overwhelms and lightens and energizes and flabbergasts all at the same time. It is the delight and privilege and birthright of every Christian.

I don't want to reach the end of my life and realize that I could have lived in a lot more grace than I did. I want to learn to recognize the call of grace. Van Morrison once sang about a certain foghorn, "I need to hear it and I don't have to fear it." I have no idea what he was talking about, but that is exactly how I feel about the language of grace, and that is the reason for this blog.

6038070R00038

Printed in Great Britain
by Amazon.co.uk, Ltd.,
Marston Gate.